ELECTRONIC STYLE

A GUIDE TO CITING ELECTRONIC INFORMATION

XIA LI AND NANCY B. CRANE

Mecklermedia
Westport • London

Fourth printing, February 1995

Library of Congress Cataloging-in-Publication Data

Li, Xia, 1964-
    Electronic style : a guide to citing electronic information / Xia
Li and Nancy B. Crane.
        p. cm.
    Includes bibliographical references (p.) and index.
    ISBN 0-88736-909-X (acid free paper) : $
    1. Bibliographical citations. 2. Data bases--Bibliography-
-Methodology. I. Crane, Nancy B. II. Title.
PN171.D37L5 1993
808'.02--dc20   93-24523
                                                        CIP

British Library Cataloguing-in-Publication Data is available.

ISBN 0-88736-909-X

Mecklermedia Corporation, 20 Ketchum Street, Westport, CT 06880.
Meckler Ltd., Artillery House, Artillery Row, London SW1P 1RT, U.K.

Printed on acid free paper.
Printed and bound in the United States of America.

ELECTRONIC
STYLE

Contents

Chapter Four: Full-Text Databases: Other Sources   25

Chapter Five: Bibliographic Databases   46

Chapter Six: Electronic Conferences (Interest Groups) or Bulletin Board Services (BBS)   49

Preface

Electronic sources are now well established as a means of information dissemination. The 1992 edition of *Computer-readable databases* has identified and verified nearly 6,800 live databases and subfiles originating from some 2,375 producers (p. ix, xi). This array of resources includes bibliographic citations, full-text files, graphic images, and numeric databases. With the striking growth in the database industry has come a parallel, and no less remarkable growth in the numbers of computer-based discussion groups and electronic periodical publishers. Worldwide, there are from 2,500 to 3,000 networked discussion lists and over 200 electronic journals, magazines, and newsletters (Strangelove and Kovacs, 1992, p. i).

Taken together, this electronic marketplace creates a new scenario for scholarship. For verification of this, one need look only as far as former President George Bush's White House, and at the legal discussion around whether to keep or erase the electronic mail archives of his administration. Scholars are placing great value on these electronic conversations. Labaton, in a recent article in the *New York Times*, says:

> . . . [U]nlike correspondence sent the old-fashioned way, the computer systems usually record the rough as well as the polished drafts, offering historians the sort of snapshot of work in progress that can illuminate the development of final documents. (1993, January 8, Sec. B, p. 14).

It should not be surprising that recurring themes of electronic discussion groups have been questions of how to cite electronic resources. What is surprising is that there is little assistance to be found to aid in the endeavor. The idea for this citation guide was born as it became clear that existing guides, such as *The MLA handbook* (1988) and the *Publication manual of the American Psychological Association* (1983), give little or no attention to these newer media.

A key to getting these resources into the mainstream is to establish a standardized approach to referencing them. *Electronic style: A guide to citing electronic information* is intended to assist in this process. It is a guide to the citation of electronic sources, and only that. It does not supply information on the mechanics of using an electronic mail system, retrieving a document from a remote site over the Internet, or searching a particular online system. Once retrieved from such a source, however, this work provides guidance in properly citing the information.

It was decided early in the process of preparing this guide that we would select a standard citation form and adapt it to include the elements that are needed to describe electronic sources. Ultimately, the citation style recommended by the American Psychological Association (APA) was chosen because: (1) the style is used widely; (2) the date, often of paramount importance in electronic sources, is given as the second element in a citation; and (3) there is great wisdom in the simple method of in-text references recommended in the APA style.

The intended audience of *Electronic style: A guide to citing electronic information* is librarians, scholars, and students, although we expect first notice to come from librarians, who are frequent mediators in the translation of information to a standard format for cited references. In time, we expect other groups to take notice—individuals whose stock-in-trade includes communicating using electronic media or who rely on information retrieved electronically.

Acknowledgments

Collecting information for this guide has been a labor of love, and at times some might have said madness. It has not been unusual for us to be seen sifting through recycle bins looking for examples that would intrigue others. A delightful discovery for us was someone else's trash. We are appreciative of the tolerance and support our colleagues in the Bailey/Howe Library Reference Department at the University of Vermont have shown during these moments, and when pitched battles erupted over brackets and parentheses!

Special thanks go to our University of Vermont colleagues William Dunlop, Laurie Kutner, Paul Philbin, and Lyman Ross who reviewed our original proposal and gave advice as the project progressed; Birdie MacLennan, who counseled us on accessing information on the Internet; and also to Jay Su at Washburn University of Topeka who gave us assistance in locating legal citations. We are thankful, too, for the unlimited access we have had to the Internet and remote sites. Vermont was one of the last states in the Union to gain access to the Internet, and without that access, collecting examples for this guide would have been impossible. Finally, the university's Office of Computing and Information Technology and the library's Systems Office, have worked wonders in connecting us to the world of high-speed communications, and have taught us the language necessary for speaking to that world.

Xia Li and Nancy B. Crane
Reference Department
Bailey/Howe Library
University of Vermont

Chapter One:

Organization and Use of this Guide

The approach taken in Chapters 2 through 8 of this guide has been to first give a "basic form" for the kind of information being cited, followed by examples using that form. These basic forms recommend the elements that should be included, and the order in which they should be presented. The basic forms are followed by real citations drawn from various sources. We have been limited by the sources to which we have access, but believe that the basic forms can be adapted to other sources.

Although this guide adheres closely to the APA style of citation, it also introduces new elements, for example: "Type of medium," and "Available" which help to better describe the newer formats. In preparing this guide it was necessary to discard some elements which are usually found in descriptions of printed sources, such as "paging," "place of publication," and even "publisher." The primary objective in making reference to an item, whether in print or electronic format, is to give enough information so that it can be located. The elements necessary to do this vary somewhat with the two formats.

The guide stresses the importance of using the "generic terms" offered by an information supplier to identify the path for retrieval of an item. The following citation, an item located using the LEXIS/NEXIS system, illustrates this approach in the "Available" statement:

Niles, T. M. T. (1992, August 17). US position and proposed actions concerning the Yugoslav crisis. *Department of State Dispatch* [Online]. Available: LEXIS Library: GENFED File: DSTATE

Individuals new to, or needing a review of the APA style, will want to read the following summary of its salient features. For a more detailed account, one can refer to the information on the "Reference List" in the *Publication manual of the American Psychological Association* (1983, pp. 111–133).

- **Author(s).** Authors are generally given as the first element of a citation, last name first, followed by the first initial of the first name and middle name, if available. When there are several authors, they are

1

all listed in the order given in the source, inverted as above, with the last author's name preceded by an ampersand, such as: Bowers, K. L., LaQuey, T., Reynolds, J., Roubicek, K., Stahl, M. & Yuan, A. If an author is lacking, the title becomes the first element of the citation.

- **Corporate Authors.** Corporate authors may replace personal authors as the first element of a citation.

- **Date.** The date is the second element of a citation, and it is enclosed in parentheses. For books, only the year of publication is given; for scholarly journal articles, year and month are given (year, month); when a magazine or newspaper article is cited, year, month and day are given (year, month day).

- **Article Title.** When an article is cited, the article title follows the date. The first word of the title is capitalized, and the first word of a subtitle. The rest of the words are not capitalized unless they are proper nouns.

- **Journal, Magazine, Newsletter, and Newspaper Titles.** The convention is to capitalize all words but articles, prepositions, and conjunctions embedded in the title. The titles are given in italics or underlined.

- **Book Titles.** The first word of titles and subtitles are capitalized, as are proper nouns. All other words begin with lowercase letters. The titles are given in italics or underlined.

- **Volume and Paging.** In the case of journals, volume and paging are given in the following manner: *volume*, paging or *55*, 12-35. If the paging is not sequential from the first issue to the last, then the issue would be given as well: *55*(4), 12-35. The volume is always given either in italics or underlined. For magazines, volumes are not given; paging is given, preceded by a "p." for a single page (p. 5), or "pp." for multiple pages (pp. 5-17).

- **Punctuation.** Main elements in citations are generally separated by periods.

- **Place of Publication: Publisher.** For books, place of publication and publisher are given, separated by a colon.

This guide adds a "Type of medium" statement, such as online, CD-ROM, or disk, directly after the name of the publication, and adds an "Available" statement, which generally replaces the information on place of publication and publisher.

Punctuation, in the context of availability statements, can present real problems. Every effort has been made to use punctuation sparingly because a stray period, comma, or slash can be mistaken for part of an address. For example, in the following item the punctuation in the "Available FTP" statement, with the exception of the colons, must be included in order to obtain the item from the supplier:

Carroll, L. (1991). *Alice's adventures in wonderland* (The Millennium Fulcrum edition 2.7a), [Online]. Available FTP: quake.think.com Directory: pub/text/1991 File: alice-in-wonderland.txt

In the example given above, all of the words in the address are given in lowercase letters. Care must be taken to duplicate upper and lowercase letters in the address or message exactly as found in the source, or reference to the source. Some computer systems are extremely sensitive to upper and lowercase letters, and if they are not supplied, the communication will fail.

The guide deviates from APA style in the section on legal sources (Chapter 4, Section II), following the advice of APA's *Publication manual...* which states that "references to legal materials will be more useful to the reader if they include the information usually contained in legal citations" (1983, p. 113). For that section, the standard guide in the legal field, *A uniform system of citation* (1991), is followed, and, as a result, citations in that section are very different from those in the rest of the guide. Wherever possible, items cited in the legal section are also listed in a section that conforms to APA style, and reference is made to that alternate form.

The last chapter presents, briefly, the author–date system of documentation recommended by APA. Comparable to footnotes or end notes in function, text references direct readers to the source of a quote or other information in a reference list at the end of an article, chapter, or book. A more detailed discussion of this method can be found in APA's *Publication manual...* in the section entitled "Reference Citations in Text" (1983, pp. 107–111).

Two appendices present information that will help in the use of this guide. Appendix I gives examples of basic availability statements for some of the more commonly used avenues for acquiring electronic information, such as DIALOG, Dow Jones News Retrieval Service, FTP, and Telnet. Appendix II is a glossary of terms that may be somewhat unfamiliar to individuals new to the world of electronic information, or have taken on new shades of meaning for the purposes of this guide.

We will close with a note about watching University of Vermont students use full-text and other electronic sources. They become acclimated quickly to the new methods of acquiring information, but some seem unsure that it is quite legitimate to cite these sources when completing final research projects. We hope that this guide, which attempts to make the citation of electronic materials a straightforward matter, will also help to legitimize their use for those who have doubts.

Chapter Two:

Full-Text Databases: Individual Works, Books, Monographs, or Full-Length Works

I. Cite an Entire Work

A. Individual Works

Basic Form
Author. (date). *Title* (edition), [Type of medium]. Available: give information sufficient for retrieval of book from supplier.

<1> *Agrochemicals handbook* [Online]. (1992, June 15). Available: Knowledge Index File: Agrochemicals Handbook (CHEM3)
  - No author is given, so the title becomes the first element of the reference, and the work is alphabetized in the reference list by the first significant word in the title; "Type of medium" statement, defining the format of this title, should precede the date.
  - If the work is under regular revision, use the date of the last revision, or if that cannot be determined, give the date on which the search was done—in the case above, "1992, June 15."

<2> *Birth defects encyclopedia online* [Online]. (1992, August). Available: BRS/After Dark File: Birth Defects Encyclopedia Online (BDEO)

<3> *The educational directory* [Online]. (1992). Available: Knowledge Index File: The Educational Directory (EDUC6)

<4> *EMBASE thesaurus* [Online]. (1991, March). Available: BRS/After Dark File: EMBASE Thesaurus (EMTH)

<5> *Kirk-Othmer online* (3rd ed.), [Online]. (1984). Available: Knowledge Index File: Kirk-Othmer Online (CHEM5)
  - An edition statement precedes the "Type of medium" statement, separated by a comma.

<6> *Mental measurements yearbook* [Online]. (1992, August). Available: BRS/After Dark File: Mental Measurements Yearbook (MMYD)

<7> *The Merck index online* [Online]. (1992, May). Available: Knowledge Index File: The Merck Index Online (DRUG4)

B. Individual Works—FTP

Basic Form
Author. (date). *Title* (edition), [Type of medium]. Available FTP: Directory: File:

<8> Carroll, L. (1991). *Alice's adventures in wonderland* (The Millennium Fulcrum edition 2.7a), [Online]. Available FTP: quake.think.com Directory: pub/etext/1991 File: alice-in-wonderland.txt

<9> Clinton, B. (1992). *Clinton/Gore on issues of concern to gays and lesbians* [Online]. Available FTP: nptn.org Directory: pub/ campaign.92/clinton.dir File: c71.txt
   • Although Clinton's first name is William, he is known as "Bill" and is cited that way.

<10> Emtage, A., Heelan, B., Rodgers, R. P. C., & Holbert, R. L. (1991). *ARCHIE (1L) manual* [Online]. Available FTP: FTP QUICHE.CS.MCGILL.CA Directory: ARCHIE/DOC File: AR-CHIE.MAN.TXT
   • This example shows the form for citing more than two authors.
   • If the source uses uppercase letters in the address, it is important that it be cited that way.

<11> Jefferson, T. (1989). *The declaration of independence* [Online]. Available FTP: quake.think.com Directory: pub/etext/1991 File: declaration-of-independence.txt
   • If a source uses lowercase letters in the address, it is important that it be cited that way.

<12> Kehoe, B. P. (1992). *Zen and the art of the Internet* (2nd ed.), [Online]. Available FTP: quake.think.com Directory: pub/etext/1992 File: zen10.txt

<13> King, M. L. (1963, August). *I have a dream* [Online]. Available FTP: mrcnext.cso.uiuc.edu Directory: gutenberg/freenet File: i-have-a-dream
  • The date given is the one included with the source.

<14> Lafayette, M. D. (1992). *Declaration of the rights of man and of the citizen* [Online]. Available FTP: mrcnext.cso.uiuc.edu Directory: gutenberg/freenet File: rights-of-man

<15> *Meeting the needs of America's women* [Speech from George Bush's Presidential Papers], [Online]. (1992, September 2). Available FTP: nptn.org Directory: pub/campaign.92/bush.dir File: b89.txt
  • This is an example of a citation for a Presidential Paper. *See also* entries 145 and 146.

C. Individual Works—Electronic Mail (e-mail)

Basic Form
Author. (date). *Title* (edition), [Type of medium]. Available e-mail: Message:

<16> Bowers, K. L., LaQuey, T., Reynolds, J., Roubicek, K., Stahl, M. & Yuan, A. (1990, August). *FYI on where to start—bibliography of Internet working information* [Online]. Available e-mail: NISINFO@NIS.NSF.NET Message: Get RFC1175.TXT-1

<17> Chew, J. J. (1991). *Inter-network mail guide* [Online]. Available e-mail: COMSERVE@RPIECS Message: Get NETWORK GUIDE

<18> Condon, C. (1990, October). *BITNET user help* [Online]. Available e-mail: NETSERV@NITNIC.BITNET Message: Get NETWORK GUIDE

<19> Gaylord, H. (1989, November). *ISO* [Online]. Available e-mail: LISTSERV@BROWNVM Message: Get ISO STANDRDS

D. Individual Works—Telnet

Basic Form
Author. (date). *Title* (edition), [Type of medium]. Available Telnet: Directory: File:

<20> *The Japanese surrender documents—WWII* [Online]. (1945, September). Available Telnet: gopher.tc.umn.edu Directory: Libraries/ Electronic Books File: Japanese Surrender

<21> *Maastricht Treaty: Treaty on European Union* [Online]. (1992, February). Available Telnet: fatty.law.cornell.edu Directory: Hong Kong, Basic Law of File: Full Text of Maastricht Treaty
   • Names of treaties are proper nouns so words are capitalized.

<22> Office of the U.S. Trade Representative. (1992). *North American Free Trade Agreement* [Online]. Available Telnet: liberty.uc.wlu.edu Directory: Nafta, synopsis–Aug 28, 1992 File: North American Free Trade Agreement

<23> *Periodic table of elements* [Online]. (1992). Available Telnet: gopher2.tc.umn.edu Directory: Libraries/Reference Works File: Periodic Table of Elements

<24> Perot, R. (1992). *An America in danger* [Online]. Available Telnet: gohper.tc.umn.edu Directory: Libraries/Electronic Books File: An America in Danger

<25> Shakespeare, W. (No date). *Hamlet* (Arthur Bullen's Stratford Town Edition), [Online]. Available Telnet: Library.Dartmouth.edu Directory: Shakespeare Plays File: Hamlet
   • Give "No date" statement if the date of publication for the work is not given in the source.

II. Cite Part of a Work

A. *Individual Works*

Basic Form
Author. (date). Title. In *Source* (edition), [Type of medium]. Available:
give information sufficient for retrieval of item from supplier.

<26> Amundson, M. E., Hart, C. A., & Holmes, T. H. (1992, March). The
schedule of recent experience. In *Mental measurements yearbook*
[Online]. Available: BRS/After Dark File: Mental Measurements
Yearbook (MMYD) Item: 1012–327

<27> Apple introduces QuickRing. (1992, May 11). In *Dow Jones News*.
[Online]. Available: Dow Jones News/Retrieval Service File:
QUICK
- No author is given, so title becomes the first element of the
  reference, and the work is alphabetized in the reference list by
  the first significant word in the title.
- In this example, *Dow Jones News* is a subfile within the
  QUICK file.

<28> Belloc, H. (1979). The early morning. In *Quotations database* [Mate-
rial from *The Oxford dictionary of quotations*, 3rd ed.], [Online].
Available: Knowledge Index File: Quotations Dictionary (REFR1)
- This is a reference to a poem from a compilation of quotations. The example gives a note in brackets that helps the
  reader identify the source of information. In this case, the online source bears a different title than the print source.

<29> Cocoa and chocolate. (1978). In *Everyman's encyclopaedia* (6th ed.),
[Online]. Available: Knowledge Index File: Everyman's Encyclo-
paedia (REFR7)
- This is an article from an encyclopedia with no author given.

<30> Gulf War vote, January 12, 1991 [Chart]. (1992). In *The almanac of
American politics* [Online], p. 1477. Available: LEXIS Library:
LEXREF File: AMPOL
- Note in brackets indicates that this information is in the form
  of a chart. *See also* entries 199 and 200.

<31> Jegede, V. A., Kowal, K. J., Lin, W., & Ritchey, M. B. (1984). Vaccine technology. In *Kirk-Othmer online* (3rd ed.), [Online], pp. 628–643. Available: Knowledge Index File: Kirk-Othmer Online (CHEM5) Item: 323270000
  • Give paging if the online source provides it.

<32> Witkop, C. J., Jr. (1990). Prime name: Albinism, oculocutaneous, Hermansky-Pudlak type. In *Birth defects encyclopedia online* [Online]. Available: BRS/After Dark File: Birth Defects Encyclopedia Online (BDEO) Item: 0033
  • The example above shows Jr. in the name.

B. Individual Works—FTP

Basic Form
Author. (date). Title. In *Source* (edition), [Type of medium]. Available FTP: Directory: File:

<33> Carroll, L. (1991). Chapter IV: The rabbit sends in a little bill. In *Alice's adventures in wonderland* (The Millennium Fulcrum edition 2.7a), [Online]. Available FTP: quake.think.com Directory: pub/etext/1991 File: alice-in-wonderland.txt

<34> Stevenson, R. L. (1992). Dr. Jekyll was quite at ease. In *Strange case of Dr. Jekyll and Mr. Hyde* (2nd Project Gutenberg etext edition), [Online]. Available FTP: mrcnext.cso.uiuc.edu Directory: etext/etext92 File: hydea10.txt

<35> Shakespeare, W. (No date). Act I. In *The Tempest* [Online]. Available FTP: quake.think.com Directory: Gutenberg/shake/Comedies/Tempest, The File: Act I
  • When no date is given with the source, it should be noted in the date statement, as shown above.

C. Individual Works—E-mail

Basic Form
Author. (date). Title. In *Source* (edition), [Type of medium]. Available e-mail: Message:

<36> Chew, J. J. (1991). How to format information for submission. In *Inter-network mail guide* [Online]. Available e-mail: COM-SERVE@RPIECS Message: Get NETWORK GUIDE

<37> Deel, N. (1992, December). Main sources for the text of United States treaties. In Georgia State University, College of Law Library, *Revision of treaties guide* [Online]. Available e-mail: law-lib%liberty.uc.wlu.edu

<38> Harnad, S. (1992). Post-Gutenberg galaxy: The fourth revolution in the means of production of knowledge. In *Directory of electronic journals, newsletters and academic discussion lists* (2nd ed.), [Online]. Available e-mail: LISTSERV@UOTTAWA Message: Get EJOURNL1 DIRECTRY

D. Individual Works—Telnet

Basic Form
Author. (date). Title. In *Source* (edition), [Type of medium]. Available Telnet: Directory: File:

<39> Norway. (1991). In *World factbook* [Online]. Available Telnet: LIBRARY.DARTMOUTH.EDU Directory: WORLD FACTBOOK File: NORWAY
   • If no author is given, the title is used as the first element of a citation.

<40> Schultes, R. E. (1991). Orchid. In *Grolier's online encyclopedia* [Online]. Available Telnet: UWIN.U.WASHINGTON.EDU Directory: I/REF/GROL File: orchid

<41> Shakespeare, W. (No date). Act I, Scene II. In *Hamlet* (Arthur Bullen's Stratford Town Edition), [Online]. Available Telnet: LIBRARY.DARTMOUTH.EDU Directory: Shakespeare plays File: Hamlet

<42> Synagogue. (1992). In *Oxford English dictionary* (2nd ed.), [Online]. Available Telnet: UWIN.U.WASHINGTON.EDU Directory: I/REF/OED File: synagogue

Chapter Three:
Full-Text Databases: Periodicals

I. Cite Part of a Work

A. *Journal Articles*

1. Journal Articles

Basic Form
Author. (year, month). Title. *Journal* [Type of medium], *volume,* paging if
given. Available: give information sufficient for retrieval of article from
supplier.

or

Author. (year, month). Title. *Journal* [Type of medium], *volume*(issue),
paging if given. Available: give information sufficient for retrieval of article from supplier.
- Issue number must be given if the paging of each issue in the
volume starts from page 1 instead of being numbered sequen-
tially throughout the volume. If paging is not given and the
source includes an issue, include that information in the
citation.

<43> Burke, J. (1992, January/February). Children's research and methods:
What media researchers are doing. *Journal of Advertising Research*
[CD-ROM], *32,* RC2–RC3. Available: UMI File: Business Periodi-
cals Ondisc Item: 92–11501
- The paging is cited exactly as given in the source.

<44> Fitzhugh, G. & Calitri, D. (1991, Spring). Kentucky experience:
Statewide mandated family life education in public schools. *Family
Life Educator* [Online], *9*(3), 10–13. Available: BRS/After Dark
File: Combined Health Information Database (CHID) Item:
HE9101117
- Capitalize the first word of a subtitle.
- Issue number must be included because the paging for each is-
sue in the volume starts with page 1.

<45> Girotti, T. B., Tweed, N. B., & Houser, N. R. (1990, February). Real-time VAr control by SCADA. *IEEE Transactions on Power Systems* [CD-ROM], *5*, 61–64. Available: UMI File: IPO (IEEE/IEE Publications Ondisc) Item: 3631953

<46> Heshusius, L. (1992). Reading meaning into texts [response to R. C. Dixon and D. W. Carnine]. *Exceptional Children* [Online], *58*, 472–476. Available: DIALOG File: Health Periodicals Database (149) Item: 11958098

<47> Horowitz, B. & Kolodny, R. (1990, May/June). Has the FASB hurt small high-technology companies? *Harvard Business Review* [Online], 44. Available: BRS/After Dark File: Harvard Business Review (HBRO) Item: 915010
  • The online version of *Harvard Business Review* has no volume or issue number; the "44" in this reference is the page number.

<48> Jacobson, M. (1988, November). Pregnancy and employment: Three approaches to equal opportunity. *Boston University Law Review* [Online], *68*, 1019ff. Available: LEXIS Library: LAWREV File: ALLREV
  • The page on which the article starts is given; the page on which the article ends in not known so the "ff" is used to indicate "and following pages."
  • *See* entry 182 for the legal citation style for this item.

<49> National Aids Information Clearinghouse. (1988, January 29). Guidelines for effective school health education to prevent the spread of AIDS. *Morbidity and Mortality Weekly Report* [Online], *37*(Suppl. S-2), 1–14. Available: BRS/After Dark File: Combined Health Information Database (CHID) Item: SA8700148
  • Alphabetize corporate authors by the first significant word in the name.

<50> Strand, D. (1991). [Review of *Behind the Tiananmen Massacre: Social, political, and economic ferment in China*]. *Political Science Quarterly* [CD-ROM], *106*, 341. Available: University Publications of America File: Scholarly Book Reviews on CD-ROM
  • If the book review is untitled, supply a title and use brackets to indicate that the information is supplied.

<51> Webb, S. L. (1992, January). Dealing with sexual harassment. *Small Business Reports* [Online], *17*, 11-14. Available: BRS File: ABI/ INFORM Item: 00591201

2. Journal Articles—FTP

Basic Form

Author. (year, month). Title. *Journal* [Type of medium], *volume*(issue), paging if given. Available FTP: Directory: File:

- Paging is seldom given in this format, so an issue becomes an important, identifying element and should be included when available.

<52> Barlow, P. (1992, June). The Joshua tree quakes. *CORE* [Online], *1* (8). Available FTP: ftp.eff.org Directory: pub/journals Files: core1.08

<53> Bridgeman, B. (1992, May). Language and plans in the analysis of consciousness: Reply to Murre on Bridgeman on consciousness. *Psycoloquy* [Online], *3*(26). Available FTP: 128.112.128.1 Directory: pub/harnad File: psyc.92.3.26.consciousness.11.bridgeman

<54> Drew, J. R. (1989, October). So that's why they call it the Big Apple. *Qyabta* [Online], *1*(1). Available FTP: export.acs.cmu.edu Directory: pub/quanta Files: quanta-oct.ps.Z

<55> Watson, L. & Dallwitz, M. J. (1990, December). Grass genera of the world - interactive identification and information retrieval. *Flora Online: An Electronic Publication of TAXACOM* [Online], (22). Available FTP: huh.harvard.edu Directory: pub/newsletters/ flora.online/issue22 File: 022gra11.txt

3. Journal Articles E-mail

Basic Form

Author. (year, month). Title. *Journal* [Type of medium], *volume*(issue), paging if given. Available e-mail: Message:

- Paging is seldom given in this format, so an issue becomes an important, identifying element and should be included when available.

<56> Chon, K. S. & Olsen, M. D. (1992, May). Functional and symbolic congruity approaches to consumer satisfaction/dissatisfaction in tourism. *Journal of the International Academy of Hospitality Research* [Online], *3*. Available: JIAHR-L@VTVM1.BITNET
  • In this example, the source does not have an issue number.

<57> Even-Zohar, I. & Harshav, B. (1988). Poetics today. *Poetics Today: International Journal for Theory and Analysis of Literature and Communication* [Online], *2*. Available e-mail: HUMAN-IST@BROWMVM Message: Get POETICS TODAY
  • In this example, the source does not give an issue number.

<58> Hardin, R. (1992, September). Dressed to kill yourself. *Postmodern Culture: An Electronic Journal of Interdisciplinary Criticism* [Online], *3*(1). Available e-mail: listserv@ncsuvm.cc.ncsu.edu Message: Get [hardin 992] pmc-list f=mail

<59> Marmion, D. (1992, July/August). Windows matures. *MeckJournal: An Electronic Monthly from Meckler Publishing* [Online], *2*(6). Available e-mail: pihl@nisc.jvnc.net

<60> Rickert, N. W. (1992, June). Consciousness and simulation. *Psycoloquy: Refereed Electronic Journal of Peer Discussion* [Online], *3* (47). Available e-mail: psyc@pucc Message: Get psyc 92–00077

<61> Rubin, C. (1992, September). Art and design slide set. *FINEART Forum* [Online], *6*(8). Available e-mail: fast@garnet.berkeley.edu
  • In this example, the availability statement does not include "Message" because it is citing a journal to which the user subscribes.

<62> Sloan, B. (1992, March). Linking OPACS: Policy issues and considerations. *MeckJournal: An Electronic Monthly from Meckler Publishing* [Online], *2*(3). Available e-mail: pihl@nisc.junc.net

<63> Winter, J. (1991) Truth as the first casualty: Mainstream media portrayal of the Gulf War. / La verite comme premiere victime. La vision de la Guerre du Golfe dans les medias dominants. *The Electronic Journal of Communication/La Revue Electronique de Communication (EJC/REC)* [Online], *2*(1). Available e-mail: Comserve@Rpiecs Message: Send Winter V2N191
  • Give all the languages in which the article title is presented.

4. Journal Articles—Telnet

Basic Form
Author. (year, month). Title. *Journal* [Type of medium], *volume*(issue), paging if given. Available Telnet: Directory: File:
- Paging is seldom given in this format, so an issue becomes an important, identifying element and should be included when available.

<64> Berch, M. C. (1992, August). Buying silence. *Quanta* [Online], *4*(3). Available Telnet: gopher.tc.umn.edu Directory: Libraries/ Newspapers, Magazines, and Newsletters/Literary Journals/Quanta/ Ascii Issues/Volume IV Issue 3 August 1992 File: "Buying Silence" by Michael C. Berch

<65> Hennequin, W. (1992, March). Sonnet to the Bichanese. *DargonZine* [Online], *5*(1). Available: gopher2.tc.umn.edu Directory: Libraries/ Newspapers, Magazines, and Newsletters/Literary Journals/ DargonZine/Vol. 5 File: N.01 03–20–92

<66> Morrison, J. (1992, January). [Review of *Comedy/Cinema/Theory*]. *Postmodern Culture* [Online], *2*(2). Available Telnet: gopher.tc.umn.edu Directory: Libraries/Newspapers, Magazines, and Newsletters/Humanities Publications/Postmondern Culture/PMC Volume 2 File: MORRISON.192
- If a book review is untitled, supply a title and enclose it in brackets, as in the example above.

<67> O'Donnell, J. J. (1992?). [Review of *The Prussian and the poet: The letters of Ulrich von Wilamowitz-Moellendorff to Gilbert Murray (1894–1930)*]. *Bryn Mawr Classical Review* [Online], *3*. Available Telnet: liberty.uc.wlu.edu Directory: Bryn Mawr Classical Review, Gopher/Volume 3 (1992) File: Bierl, A., Calder, W. M., and Fowler, R., *The Prussian and the Poet...
- "Supplied titles" should be given in brackets.
- If uncertain of the date, give the date with a question mark to indicate that uncertainty.

B. Magazine Articles

1. Magazine Articles

Basic Form

Author. (year, month day). Title. *Magazine* [Type of medium], paging if given. Available: give information sufficient for retrieval of article from supplier.

<68> Church, G. J. (1990, Fall). The view from behind bars: The number of women inmates tripled in the past decade. Most of them are mothers. They face a system designed and run by men for men. [Special issue: Women, the road ahead]. *Time* [Online], pp. 20–22. Available: DIALOG File: Magazine ASAP (647) Item: 09012630
  • It is important to indicate that an item is from a special issue of a publication. In the case above, this information is enclosed in brackets following the article title.

<69> Dortch, M. (1992, June 1). Netware for giant LANS approaches: Novell says next release. *CommunicationsWeek* [CD-ROM], pp. 1–2. Available: Ziff Communications Co. File: Computer Select Item: 12 235 992

<70> Dwyer, V. (1991, July 29). [Review of *Boyz N the Hood*]. *MacLean's* [Online], p. 47. Available: DIALOG File: Magazine ASAP (647) Item: 11064060
  • "Supplied titles" are given in brackets.

<71> Exercise helps clear fat from bloodstream. (1990, June). *HeartCare* [CD-ROM], p. 13. Available: InfoTrac File: Health Reference Center

<72> Fujie, S. & Mikami, Y. (1991, April). Construction aspects of intelligent buildings. *IEEE Communications Magazine* [CD-ROM], pp. 50–57. Available: UMI File: IPO (IEEE/IEE Publications Ondisc) Item: 3939837

<73> LaRosa, S. M. (1992, March). Marketing slays the downsizing dragon. *Information Today* [CD-ROM], pp. 58–59. Available: UMI File: Business Periodicals Ondisc Item: 92–20889

<74> Niles, T. M. T. (1992, August 17). US position and proposed actions concerning the Yugoslav crisis. *Department of State Dispatch* [Online]. Available: LEXIS Library: GENFED File: DSTATE

<75> Technology projections: 2001. (1992, May). *Direct Marketing* [CD-ROM], pp. 23–25. Available: UMI File: Business Periodicals On-disc Item: 92–29833

<76> Youngwood, S. (1992, February). Book publishers proliferate in Vermont. *Vermont Business Magazine* [CD-ROM], Sec. 1, p. 25. Available: UMI File: Business Dateline Ondisc Item: 92–18178

<77> Zinsmeister, K. (1990, June). Growing up scared: Spurred on by family instability, violent crime now touches millions of young lives. *Atlantic* [Online], pp. 49–62. Available: DIALOG File: Magazine ASAP (647) Item: 09051271

2. Magazine Articles—FTP

Basic Form
Author. (year, month day). Title. *Magazine* [Type of medium], paging if given. Available FTP: Directory: File:

<78> Quin, L. R. E. (1990). Summary of meta fonts available. *TeXMag* [Online]. Available FTP: sun.soe.clarkson.edu Directory: pub/tex/texmag File: texmag.4.06

<79> Rosenthol, L. (1992, December 24). Apple SOS service is amazing! *Info-Mac Digest* [Online]. Available FTP: sumex-aim.stanford.edu Directory: Volume1/info-mac/digest/im File: informacv10–305.txt

3. Magazine Articles—E-mail

Basic Form
Author. (year, month day). Title. *Magazine* [Type of medium], paging if given. Available e-mail: Message:

<80> Flaherty, T. (1988, August 26). Compendium of genealogical software. *Humanist Mailing List* [Online], 2(43). Available e-mail: HUMANIST@BROWNVM Message: Get GENEALGY REPORT

<81> Rubenstein, B. (1989, April 17). 1988 directory of computer assisted research in musicology. *Music Research Digest* [Online]. Available

e-mail: HUMANIST@BROWNVM Message: Get MUSIC DI-
GEST

<82> Truck, F. (1992, June). [Abstract of *Archaeopteryx*]. *Art Com* [On-
line]. Available e-mail: artcometv@well.sf.ca.us
- *See* entry 84 which is a reference to the same item acquired
from a remote site (Telnet).

4. Magazine Articles—Telnet

Basic Form
Author. (year, month day). Title. *Magazine* [Type of medium]. Available
Telnet: Directory: File:

<83> O'Donnell, D. B. (1990, July). Memories of blue. *Athene-InerText:
The Online Magazine of Amateur Creative Writing* [Online]. Avail-
able Telnet: gopher.unt.edu Directory: Literary Anthologies/
Athene-Intertext/Athene File: V.2 I.3 Jul 90

<84> Truck, F. (1992, June). [Abstract of *Archaeopteryx*]. *Art Com* [On-
line]. Available Telnet: gopher.tc.umn.edu Directory: Libraries/
Newspapers, Magazines, and Newsletters/Art/Art Com File: V.1
N.3 Jun 92
- *See* entry 82 which is a reference to the same item acquired
via e-mail.

C. Newsletter Articles

1. Newsletter Articles

Basic Form
Author. (year, month day). Title. *Newsletter* [Type of medium], paging if
given. Available: File: Item:

<85> For Hands That Do Work [Product name from *Weekly Trademark Re-
view*). (1992, January 13). *The Rose Sheet* [Online], p. 16. Available: BRS/After Dark File: FDC Reports (FDCR) Item: 0213002105
- Capitals used in the title of the article because this is the name
of a product.

<86> Langseth, L. (1989, November). Caffeine and cholesterol: Two reports. *Nutrition Research Newsletter* [CD-ROM], pp. 123–124. Available: Information Access Company (InfoTrac) File: Health Reference Center

<87> St. Paul's College likely to pick energy answers for integrated waste plant. (1991, October 11). *Integrated Waste Management* [Online], p. 5. Available: NEXIS Library: ENERGY File: IWM

<88> Silicone gel breast implant recall urged by health research group; Consumer group finds noncompliance with FDA's breast implant moratorium request. (1992, January 20). *The Gray Sheet* [Online], p. 7. Available: BRS/After Dark File: FDC Reports (FDCR) Item: 0118003002

2. Newsletter Articles—FTP

Basic Form
Author. (year, month day). Title. *Newsletter* [Type of medium], paging if given. Available FTP: Directory: File:

<89> Marine, A. (1992, July/August). How did we get 727,000 hosts? *CERFNet News*, [Online]. Available FTP: nic.cerf.net Directory: CERFNet/CERFNet News File: july/august

<90> Ray, M. S. (1992, March 27). Conference: Solid waste management & secondary materials. *Che Electronic Newsletter*, [Online]. Available FTP: cc.curtin.edu.au Directory: chemeng/1992/july-august File: july-august.txt

<91> DEC Triumph. (1992, December). *Vaporware: H.U.G.E Apple Club (E. Hartford) News Letter* [Online]. Available FTP: sumex-aim.stanford.edu Directory: Volume/info-mac/digest/vapor File: vaporware-12–92.txt

3. Newsletter Articles—E-mail

Basic Form
Author. (year, month day). Title. *Newsletter* [Type of medium], paging if given. Available e-mail: Message:

<92> Hart, M. (1992, July 31). The newest Project Gutenberg FTP site is at Cleveland Freenet! *Project Gutenberg Newsletter* [Online]. Available e-mail: PACS-L@UHUPVM1. BITNET
  • This newsletter is disseminated by subscription, so there is no "Message" segment.

<93> Lynch, C. (1992, May). [Review of *Mirror worlds, or, the day software puts the universe in a shoebox*]. *Current Cites* [Online]. Available e-mail: PACS-L@UHUPVM1.BITNET
  • The supplied title is given in brackets.

<94> Kondor, R. (1992, May 10). Hebrew as a second language (PC). *Electronic Hebrew Users Newsletter* [Online]. Available e-mail: listserv@dartcms1 Message: Get E-HUG 92–00019

<95> O'Neill, K. (1992, August 18). Database update. *Comserve News*, [Online]. Available e-mail: Comserve@Rpiecs

<96> Owen, D. (1989, April 25). APA electronic texts in philosophy initiative. *Offline*, [Online]. Available: e-mail: listserv@brownvm Message: get APA_PHIL ETEXTS

<97> Quint, B. (1992, May 13). Wedding announcements [editorial]. *Public-Access Computer Systems News* [Online]. Available e-mail: PACS-L@UHUPVM1.BITNET
  • This is an example of a citation for an editorial.

<98> Zhao, H. Q. (1992, August 11). Chinese Student Protection Act of 1992, S1216. *China News Digest (US News)*, [Online]. Available e-mail: CHINA-ND@KENTVM.BITNET

4. Newsletter Articles—Telnet

Basic Form
Author. (year, month day). Title. *Newsletter* [Type of medium]. Available Telnet: Directory: File:

<99> James, J. S. (1992, September 18). Alpha-APA: New anti-HIV compound. *AIDS Treatment News* [Online]. Available: gopher.tc.umn.edu Directory: Libraries/Newspapers, Magazines, and Newsletters/Medical Publications/AIDS News File: Issue 159 08–19–92

<100> Paris club defers CIS debt until 30 June. (1992, April 1). *News of Earth: Global News Monitored from Shortwave Radio Broadcasts* [Online]. Available Telnet: gopher.unt.edu Directory: News From Earth/1992 File: 04–01–92 Issue 04

<101> Ray, J. W. (1992, July). Hot air about the atmosphere?. *ECIX Climate Digest* [Online]. Available Telnet: gopher.unt.edu Directory: Science/Canadian Global Change Newsletters File: climdig9_jul92

<102> Taylor, C. (1992, August 10). Reflections on windows word processing. *Buffer: The Newsjournal of Computing at the University of Denver* [Online]. Available Telnet: du.edu Directory: buffer/ 08–1992 File: windows

D. Newspaper Articles

Basic Form
Author. (year, month day). Title. *Newspaper* [Type of medium], edition, section, paging if given. Available: give information sufficient for retrieval of article from supplier.

<103> Bronner, E. (1990, October 31). Souter voices concern over abortion curb. *Boston Globe* [Online], National/Foreign, p. 1. Available: DIALOG File: Boston Globe (631) Item: 05805028

<104> Faison, S., Jr. (1992, February 1). Summit at the U.N.; Bush and Chinese Prime Minister meet briefly at U.N. amid protests. *The New York Times* [CD-ROM], Late Edition, Sec. 1: Foreign Desk, p. 1. Available: UMI File: New York Times Ondisc Item: 9200014094
  • This example shows how to cite "Jr." as part of a name.

<105> Maslin, J. (1992, March 20). Review/film; Dissension in the ranks of a household's 4 wives [Review of *Raise the red lantern*]. *The New York Times* [CD-ROM], Late Edition, Sec. C: Weekend Desk, p. 18. Available: UMI File: New York Times OnDisc Item: 9200023548
  • This is a citation to a review of a film. The name of the film is provided, enclosed in brackets to indicate that the information is not part of the title of the review.

<106> Meadows, D. H. (1988, July 31). The greenhouse down to earth. *Los Angeles Times* [Online], Home Edition, Opinion, p. 1. Available: Knowledge Index File: Los Angeles Times (NEWS10) Item: 00826693

<107> Perlman, E. (1992, June 1/June 14). House, Senate far apart on urban package: Special report. *City & State* [Online], p. 3. Available: NEXIS Library: NEXIS File: CTY&ST
  • Two dates are associated with this issue.

<108> Reinke, M. (1992, March 23). Kid's treat: Ice cream-loving family finds new niche at mall. *The Business Journal-Phoenix & the Valley of the Sun* [CD-ROM], Sec. 1, p. 1. Available: UMI File: Business Dateline Item: 9227912

<109> Rodgers, W. A. (1992, April 6). Quail Ridge Lodge targets hunters, business leaders. *Greater Cincinnati Business Record* [CD-ROM], Sec. 1, p. 7. Available: UMI File: Business Dateline Item: 9230944

<110> Special voters' guide to state and local elections; Congressional races; District 23. (1992, October 25). *Los Angeles Times* [Online], Special Section, Pt. T, p. 6. Available: NEXIS Library: NEXIS File: LAT
  • This is an example of an article from a special section of a newspaper.

<111> Tooshoos, G. (1992, December 7). Problems are not od *[sic]*. *Minnesota Daily* [Online]. Available Telnet: gopher.tc.umn.edu Directory: Libraries/Newspaper, Magazines, and Newsletters/Campus Newspapers/Minnesota Daily File: Search 1992/1993 School Year
  • This article was obtained from a remote site (Telnet).

<112> Wilson J. (1990, May 10). Portable landscape container gardens can add splashes of color, allow plants to follow the sun and give gardeners more space. *San Jose Mercury News* [Online], Morning Edition, Garden, p. 1E. Available: Knowledge Index File: San Jose Mercury News (NEWS11) Item: 05631297

II. Cite an Entire Work

Basic Form
Periodical Title [Type of medium]. Available: give information sufficient for
retrieval of item from supplier.

<113> *Asian Wall Street Journal Weekly* [Online]. Available: LEXIS Li-
brary: ASIAPC File: AWS
  • Citation to an entire newspaper from a commercial source.

<114> *CORE* [Online]. Available FTP: ftp.eff.org Directory: pub File:
journals
  • Reference to a journal from a remote site (FTP).

<115> *Electronic Hebrew Users Newsletter* (E-HUG), [Online]. Available
e-mail: listserv@dartcms1 Message: index E-HUG
  • Reference to a newsletter from a remote site (e-mail).

<116> *Forbes* [Online]. Available: NEXIS Library: MAGS File: FORBES
  • Citation to a magazine from a commercial source.

<117> *Health News Daily* [Online]. Available: BRS/After Dark File:
Health Daily News (HNDY)
  • Citation to a newsletter from a commercial source.

<118> *Journal of Consumer Research* [Online]. Available: NEXIS Library:
MARKET File: JCONRS
  • Citation to a journal from a commercial source.

<119> *Minnesota Daily* [Online]. Available Telnet: gopher.tc.umn.edu Di-
rectory: Libraries/Newspapers, Magazines, and Newsletters/
Campus Newspapers File: Minnesota Daily
  • Citation to a newspaper from a remote site (Telnet).

<120> *PSYCOLOQUY: Refereed Electronic Journal of Peer Discussion*
[Online]. Available e-mail: psyc@pucc Message: get psyc 92–
00077
  • Citation to a journal from a remote site (e-mail).

<121> *This Week at Gettysburg (TWAG)*, [Online]. Available Telnet: go-
pher.tc.umn.edu Directory: Libraries/Newspapers, Magazines, and
Newsletters/Campus Newspapers File: This Week at Gettysburg
(TWAG)
  • Citation to a newsletter from a remote site (Telnet).

Chapter Four:

Full-Text Databases: Other Sources

I. United States Government Documents

A. Bills, Resolutions

Basic Form
Legislative body. Number of Congress, Session. (year, month day). *Number of bill or resolution, Title* [Type of medium]. Available: give information sufficient for retrieval of item from supplier.

<122> U.S. House. 102nd Congress, 1st Session. (1991, January 11). *H. Con. Res. 1, Sense of the Congress on Approval of Military Action Against Iraq* [Online]. Available: LEXIS Library: GENFED File: BILLS
  - Words in the names of bills and resolutions should be capitalized as indicated in the electronic source.
  - *See* entry 155 for the legal citation style for this item.

<123> U.S. House. 102nd Congress, 1st Session. (1991, October 29). *H. J. Res. 365, To Designate the Provasoli-Guillard Center for the Culture of Marine Phytoplankton as a National Center and Facility* [Online]. Available: LEXIS Library: GENFED File: BILLS
  - *See* entry 156 for the legal citation style for this item.

<124> U.S. House. 102nd Congress, 2nd Session. (1992, October 1). *H. R. 6089, A Bill to Restructure the Federal Budget Process* [Provides line item veto rescission authority], [Online]. Available: LEXIS Library: GENFED File: BILLS
  - A note providing a description of content is placed in brackets.
  - *See* entry 157 for the legal citation style for this item.

<125> U.S. Senate. 102nd Congress, 2nd Session. (1992, May 1). *S. 2403, A Bill to Rescind Certain Budget Authority Proposed to Be Rescinded in Special Messages Transmitted to the Congress by the President on March 20, 1992, in Accordance with Title X of the Congressional Budget and Impoundment Control Act of 1974, as Amended* [Online]. Available: LEXIS Library: GENFED File: BILLS
  - *See* entry 158 for the legal citation style for this item.

<126> U.S. Senate. 102nd Congress, 1st Session. (1991, October 26). *S. J. Res. 220, To Designate the Provasoli-Guillard Center for the Culture of Marine Phytoplankton as a National Center and Facility* [Online]. Available: LEXIS Library: GENFED File: BILLS
- *See* entry 159 for the legal citation style for this item.

B. Census

Basic Form
Title [Type of medium]. (date). Available: give information sufficient for retrieval of item from supplier.

<127> *Asian or Pacific Islander females* [CD-ROM]. (1990). Available: 1990 Census of Population and Housing Summary Tape File 3A Path: Vermont/Burlington, VT MSA/Race by sex by age File: Asian or Pacific Islander females
- This is a reference to a file within a database.

Examples of the same item acquired by different paths:

<128> *U.S. Census, 1990: Census of population and housing* [Online]. (1990). Available e-mail: hart@vmd.cso.uiuc.edu Message: Get uscen90.txt

<129> *U.S. Census, 1990: Census of population and housing* [Online]. (1990). Available FTP: mrcnext.cso.uiuc.edu Directory: etext/etext91 File: uscen90.txt

<130> *U.S. Census, 1990: Census of population and housing* [Online]. (1990). Available Telnet: liberty.uc.wlu.edu Select: to legal sources File: The 1990 United States Census
- Once a user gets to a Telnet site, an action is selected which results in the location of a file.

C. Code of Federal Regulations

Basic Form
Name of Section. (date). *Code of Federal Regulations* [Type of medium], *Title (Tit.) number*, Part (Pt.) number. Available: give information sufficient for retrieval of item from supplier.

<131> Land and Water: Operation and Maintenance. (1992). *Code of Federal Regulations* [Online], *Tit. 25*, Pt. 171. Available: LEXIS Library: CODES File: CFR
  • *See* entry 185 for the legal citation style for this item.

D. Congressional Record

Basic Form
Last name of speaker, title, abbreviated [home state]. (year, month day). Title. *Congressional Record* [Type of medium], *volume*, paging. Available: give information sufficient for retrieval of item from supplier.

<132> Waxman, Rep. [CA]. (1992, August 6). Conference report on S. 323, Family Planning Amendments Act of 1992. *Congressional Record* [Online], *138*, p. H7686. Available: LEXIS Library: LEGIS File: RECORD
  • The *Congressional Record* does not give initials of speakers as a rule so the initial(s) is (are) replaced with title: Representative (Rep.) or Senator (Sen.).

E. Federal Register

Basic Form
Title or name of the section (agency report number if given). (year, month day). *Federal Register* [Type of medium], *volume*, starting page. Available: give information sufficient for retrieval of item from supplier.

<133> Initial list of categories of sources under Section 112(c)(1) of the Clean Air Amendments of 1990 (FRL-4152-7). (1992, July 16). *Federal Register* [Online], *57*, p. 31576. Available: NEXIS Library: EXEC File: FEDREG
  • Provide the report number, if given, in parentheses immediately following the title.
  • See entry 186 for the legal citation style for this item.

<134> Availability of the draft environmental assessment and land protection plan; Proposed established [*sic*] of Grand Bay National Wildlife Refuge Jackson County, MS and Mobile County, AL (Notice). (1992, January 21). *Federal Register* [CD-ROM], *57*, p. 2284. Available: Counterpoint Publishing File: Federal Register

- In this example, there is an obvious typographical error in the title. The item is entered *exactly* as it appears in the source with the indication [*sic*] that the writer has noted that error but is presenting the information as found.

F. House or Senate Reports

Basic Form
Legislative body. Number of Congress, Session. (date). *Title* (House/Senate Report number), [Type of medium]. Available: give information sufficient for retrieval of item from supplier.

<135> U.S. House. 102nd Congress, 2nd Session. (1992). *Family and Medical Leave Act of 1992* (House Report 102–816), [Online]. Available: LEXIS Library: GENFED File: CMTRPT
  - The report number from the online source varies somewhat from the way it might look if taken from a printed source. In the latter case, the item would be cited as: *102–2, House Report 816*, referring to the Congress number (102), session number (2), branch of Congress (House) and report number (816).

<136> U.S. Senate. 102nd Congress, 1st Session. (1991). *Older Americans Act Reauthorization Amendments of 1991: Conference Report to Accompany S. 243* (Senate Report 102–51), [Online]. Available: LEXIS Library: LEGIS File: CMTRPT

G. National Trade Data Bank (NTDB)

Basic Form
Author. (date). *Title* (edition), [Type of medium]. Available: give information sufficient for retrieval of item from supplier.

<137> Office of the U.S. Trade Representative. (1992, October 2). *Lack of intellectual property protection* [Japan], [CD-ROM]. Available: National Trade Data Bank—The Export Connection (R) Program: National Trade Estimate Report on Foreign Trade Barriers Title: 4. Lack of Intellectual Property Protection
  - If an important element to make the entry clear is lacking, provide that information in a note enclosed in brackets.

- When indicating the availability, use the generic category names as they are given in the database. In this example, use "Program" and "Title" instead of the usual "Directory" and "File."

<138> U.S. Department of State. (1992, October 2). *Luthuania economic policy and trade practices* [CD-ROM]. Available: National Trade Data Bank—The Export Connection (R) Program: Country Reports on Economic Policy and Trade Practices Title: Luthuania Economic Policy and Trade Practices

<139> Bureau of the Census. (1992, October 2). *Commercial banking* [U.S. industrial outlook, 1992], [CD-ROM]. Available: National Trade Data Bank—The Export Connection (R) Program: U.S Industrial Outlook, 1992 Title: CHAP46 Commercial Banking
- If the title does not indicate the contents clearly, provide the program as a note in brackets after the title.

<140> International Trade Administration. (1992, October 2). *Foreign labor trend report: Hungary 1991–1992* [CD-ROM]. Available: National Trade Data Bank—The Export Connection (R) Program: Market Research Reports Title: Hungary—Foreign Labor Trend 1981–92 - FLT9207

H. Patents

Basic Form
Name of the invention, by inventor's name. (year, month day). *Patent Number* [Type of medium]. Available: give information sufficient for retrieval of item from supplier.
- When citing patents, the most important element is the name of the invention, which is given first, followed by the inventor's name.

<141> Apple tree "Vermont Gold", by W. H. Luginbuhl. (1991, August 13). *Patent PP 7618* [Online]. Available: NEXIS Library: PATENT File: PLANT
- The date given is the date the patent was issued rather than the application date.

<142> Compact Cortland apple tree – LaMont cultivar, by G. LaMont.
(1982, January 19). *Patent PP 4800* [Online]. Available: NEXIS
Library: PATENT File: PLANT

<143> Musical toothbrush with adjustable neck and mirror, by L. M. R.
Brooks. (1992, May 19). *Patent D 326,189* [Online]. Available:
NEXIS Library: LEXPAT File: DESIGN

I. Periodicals

Basic Form

Author. (year, month day). Title. *Magazine* [Type of medium], paging if
given. Available: give information sufficient for retrieval of article from
supplier.

<144> Niles, T. M. T. (1992, August 17). US position and proposed actions
concerning the Yugoslav crisis. *Department of State Dispatch*
[Online]. Available: LEXIS Library: GENFED File: DSTATE

J. Presidential Papers

Basic Form

Title [Nature of document, e.g., proclamation, speech, date]. (Date of publication). *Weekly Compilation of Presidential Documents* [Online], *volume*,
paging. Available: give information sufficient for retrieval of item from
supplier.

<145> Statement on the United Nations Security Council vote on humanitar-
ian aid to Bosnia [Speech]. (1992, August 13). *Weekly Compilation of Presidential Documents* [Online], *28*, 1436. Available:
LEXIS Library: GENFED File: PRESDC
- In this example, the date of the speech and publication are one
in the same, so only the publication date is given. If the dates
were different, the date might be given in the title or in the
statement identifying the nature of the document, e.g.,
[Speech, August 8, 1992].
- The name of the president, as author, is unnecessary because
the date identifies the administration.

<146> Helping small businesses to grow and create jobs [Speech from
George Bush's Presidential Papers], [Online]. (1992, August 12).

Available FTP: nptn.org Directory: pub/campaign.92/bush.dir
File: b28.txt
- This is an example of a presidential speech transferred from a
  remote site (FTP).

K. U.S. Code

Basic Form
Title of section. (date). *Version of code* [Type of medium], Title (Tit.) number, Section (Sec.) number. Available: give information sufficient for retrieval of item from supplier.

<147> Chinese Student Protection Act of 1992. (1992). *United States Code
Annotated* [Online], Tit. 8, Sec. 1255 Note. Available: WEST-
LAW Database: US-PL
- Use the terms given by the information supplier to show the
  path used to get the information, e.g., "Database" instead
  "File."
- *See* entry 163 for the legal citation style for this item.

<148> Disaster Relief Miscellaneous. (1992). *United States Code Service*
[Online], Tit. 42, Sec. 5204(a). Available: LEXIS Library:
CODES File: USCODE
- *See* entry 164 for the legal citation style for this item.

L. U.S. Constitution

Basic Form
Title of section. (date). *Version of Constitution* [Type of medium], Article
and section numbers. Available: give information sufficient for retrieval
of item from supplier.

<149> *The Constitution of the United States* [Online], Amendment 1.
(1992). Available FTP: oes.orst.edu Directory: bin/compress
File: us-const
- In this example, the version of the Constitution is not named,
  nor is the title of the amendment given.
- *See* entry 187 for the legal citation style for this item.

<150> Right to bear arms. (1992). *United States Code Service: Constitution
of the United States of America* [Online], Amendment 2. Available: LEXIS Library: GENFED File: USCNST
- *See* entry 188 for the legal citation style for this item.

M. U.S. Reports (Supreme Court Decisions)

Basic Form

Full name of case. (year, month day). *United States Reports* [Type of medium], *volume*, page(s). Available: give information sufficient for retrieval of item from supplier.

<151> Regents of the University of California v. Bakke. (1978, June 28). *United States Reports* [Online], *438*, 265. Available: LEXIS Library: GENFED File: US
  • *See* entry 180 for the legal citation style for this item.

N. U.S. Statutes at Large

Basic Form

Title of Act, Public Law (PL) Number. (date). *United States Statutes at Large* [Type of medium], *volume*, page. Available: Give information sufficient for retrieval of item from supplier.

<152> Act of October 28, 1991, PL 102–143. (1991). *United States Statutes at Large* [Online], *105*, 917. Available: LEXIS Library: LEGIS File: PUBLAW
  • The text of this public law is untitled.
  • *See* entry 166 for the legal citation style for this item.

<153> Act of November 21, 1991 To Amend the Civil Rights Act of 1964, PL 102–166. (1991). *United States Statutes at Large* [Online], *105*, 1071. Available: LEXIS Library: GENFED File: USCODE
  • *See* entry 167 for the legal citation style for this item.

<154> Chinese Student Protection Act of 1992, PL 102–404. (1992). *United States Statutes at Large* [Online], *106*, 1969. Available: WESTLAW Database: US-PL
  • *See* entry 168 for the legal citation style for this item.

II. Legal Sources

Legal citation style varies significantly from APA style. The accepted practice in legal citation is to cite references in footnotes. *The publication manual of the American Psychological Association* indicates that "references to legal materials will be more useful to the reader if they include the information usually contained in legal citations" (1983, p. 113). They recommend that *A uniform system of citation* be used as a guide when citing legal sources. That recommendation has been followed in this section. However, we have consistently added names—for bills, sections of codes, and cases. This practice differs from *A uniform system...*, but generally makes it easier for others to locate a cited item in an electronic source.

A. Bills, Resolutions

Basic Form
Title, Bill, or Resolution number, Congress, Session. (date) (Give information sufficient for retrieval of item).

<155> Sense of the Congress on Approval of Military Action Against Iraq, H. Con. Res. 1, 102nd Cong., 1st Sess. (1991) (LEXIS, Genfed, Bills).
  • For a citation using APA style, *see* entry 122.

<156> To Designate the Provasoli-Guillard Center for the Culture of Marine Phytoplankton as a National Center and Facility, H. J. Res. 365, 102nd Cong., 1st Sess. (1991) (LEXIS, Genfed, Bills).
  • For a citation using APA style, *see* entry 123.

<157> A Bill to Restructure the Federal Budget Process, H. R. 6089, 102nd Cong., 2nd Sess. (1992) (LEXIS, Genfed, Bills).
  • For a citation using APA style, *see* entry 124.

<158> A Bill to Rescind Certain Budget Authority Proposed to Be Rescinded in Special Messages Transmitted to the Congress by the President on March 20, 1992, in Accordance with Title X of the Congressional Budget and Impoundment Control Act of 1974, as Amended, S. 2403, 102nd Cong., 2nd Sess. (1992) (LEXIS, Genfed, Bills).
  • For a citation using APA style, *see* entry 125.

<159> To Designate the Provasoli-Guillard Center for the Culture of Marine Phytoplankton as a National Center and Facility, S. J. Res. 220, 102 Cong., 1st Sess. (1991) (LEXIS, Genfed, Bills).
  • For a citation using APA style, *see* entry 126.

B. Codes of Law, Statutes

Basic Form
Official or Popular Name (or both), Title number Title of code Section (\S\) number (date) (Give information for retrieval of item).

1. State Codes

Basic Form
The proper citation form for state codes of law varies from state to state and with reporting service. A few examples are given below to show this variation. Consult *A uniform system of citation* for a complete guide to the form(s) for each state.

<160> Application, Administration and Enforcement of Wildlife Laws: General Provisions, Or. Rev. Stat. \S\ 496.004 (1991) (LEXIS, Codes, Orcode).

<161> Assessment of Local Taxes: Personal Estate, Where and To Whom Assessed, Mass. Ann. Laws ch. 59, \S\ 18 (Law. Co-op. 1991) (LEXIS, Codes, Macode).

<162> Vermont Water Resources Board: Duties and Powers, Vt. Stat. Ann. tit. 10, \S\ 905 (1991) (LEXIS, Codes, Vtcode).

2. U.S. Code

<163> Chinese Student Protection Act of 1992, 8 U.S.C.A. \S\ 1255 Note (1992) (WESTLAW, US-PL).
  • For a citation using APA style, *see* entry 147.

<164> Disaster Relief Miscellaneous, 42 U.S.C.S. \S\ 5204(a) (Lawyers Co-op 1992) (LEXIS, Codes, UScode).

- This is a reference to the *United States Code Service* (Lawyers Co-op).
- For a citation using APA style, *see* entry 148.

<165> Patent Act, 35 U.S.C.S. \S\ 1–376 (Lawyers Co-op no date) (Telnet: fatty.law.cornell.edu Select: to legal sources File: Patent Act)
- If the reference does not have a date, give "no date" in place of the date.

3. U.S. Statutes at Large

Basic Form
Title of Act, Pub. L. No. volume Stat. page (date) (Give information sufficient for retrieval of item).

<166> Act of October 28, 1991, Pub. L. No. 102–143, 105 Stat. 917 (1991) (LEXIS, Legis, Publaw).
- The text of this public law is untitled.
- For a citation using APA style, *see* entry 152.

<167> Act of November 21, 1991 To Amend the Civil Rights Act of 1964, Pub. L. No. 102–166, 105 Stat. 1071 (1991) (LEXIS, Genfed, UScode).
- For a citation using APA style, *see* entry 153.

<168> Chinese Student Protection Act of 1992, Pub. L. No. 102–404, 106 Stat. 1969 (1992) (WESTLAW, US-PL).
- For a citation using APA style, *see* entry 154.

C. Court Decisions

Basic Form
Name of case, Source(s) using legal citation style, (date) (Give information sufficient for retrieval of item).

1. State Courts

<169> General Telephone Company of California v. Public Utilities Commission; City of Santa Monica, Real Party in Interest, 34 Cal. 3d 817, 670 P.2d 349, 195 Cal. Rptr. 695 (1983) (LEXIS, Cal, Cal).

- The practice is to cite all of the decision-reporting services, whenever possible.

<170> Leon Devince Kerney, v. State of Florida, 1992 WL 220515, (Fla. App. 2 Dist.), 17 Fla. L. Week. D2137 (1992) (WESTLAW, All-states).

2. U.S. Court of Appeals

<171> Karen Lynn Williams, Kenneth Williams v. Heavenly Valley, 1991 U.S. App. LEXIS 24940 (9th Cir. 1991) (LEXIS, Genfed, USapp).
- This is an example of a recent decision cited from a computerized legal source before a citation for the official source is available.

<172> Stephen L. Gray v. Michael T. O'Brien and the Sugarloaf Mountain Corporation, 777 F.2d (1st Cir. 1985) (LEXIS, Genfed, USapp).
- This is an example of a page citation, in this case to page 864, 865.

<173> Sylvio J. Pitasi and Joan Pitasi v. Stratton Corporation, 968 F. 2d 1558, 1992 U.S. App LEXIS 16051 (2nd Cir. 1992) (LEXIS, Genfed, USapp).
- The above gives an example of citing both the official and a computerized legal source for a recently decided case.

<174> United States of America v. Daniel B. Hughes, a/k/a "Sonny", 716 F.2d 234 (4th Cir. 1983) (WESTLAW, Allfeds).

3. U.S. District Courts

<175> Louisiana Power and Light Company v. United Gas Pipe Line Company, 642 F. Supp. 781 (E.D. La. 1986) (LEXIS, Genfed, Dist).
- Check *A uniform system...* for the standard form of entry for individual states. For example, note the variation in the following: Alaska—Alaska; Louisiana—La.; Michigan—Mich.; New York—N.Y.
- It is important to give the district from which a case was heard, in this instance Eastern District, Louisiana, which is abbreviated as "E.D. La."

<176> Town of Springfield, Vermont and Vermont Public Power Supply
Authority v. State of Vermont Environment Board, Concerned Citizens of the Black River Valley and Town of Cavendish, 521 F.
Supp. 243 (D. Vt. 1981) (LEXIS, Genfed, Dist).

<177> United Paperworkers International Union v. International Paper Company, 1992 U.S. Dist. LEXIS 12583 (S.D. N.Y. Aug. 17, 1992)
(LEXIS, Genfed, Dist).

<178> United States of America v. Exxon Corporation and Exxon Shipping
Company, No. A90–015 CR (D. Alaska, filed Feb. 27, 1990)
(LEXIS, Genfed, Dist).
- If the date is not that of a decision, indicate in parentheses
  what the date cited is. In this example, the date given is the
  date the case was filed with the court.

4. U.S. Supreme Court

<179> Planned Parenthood of Southeastern Pennsylvania v. Casey Health
Care, U.S.L.W.D., No. 91–744 (U.S. June 29, 1992) (LEXIS, Genfed, USlwd).
- Generally the advice is to use a looseleaf service citation only
  until the case is available in an official or Supreme Court reporting service.
- This example is from the *U.S. Law Week—Daily Edition*. The
  reference case gives a docket number for easy identification,
  and indicates that the decision was rendered by the Supreme
  Court on a particular date.

<180> Regents of the University of California v. Bakke, 438 U.S. 265, 98 S.
Ct. 2733, 1978 U.S. LEXIS 5, 57 L. Ed. 2d 750, (1978) (LEXIS,
Genfed, US).
- This example gives citations for all of the major Supreme
  Court reporting services.
- For a citation using APA style, *see* entry 151.

<181> Republic National Bank of Miami v. United States, No. 91–767
(1992) (Telnet: fatty.law.cornell.edu Directory: Supreme Court
Decision File: Republic National...).

D. Periodicals

Basic Form

Author, *Title*, volume Journal page (date) (Give information sufficient for retrieval of item).

- APA style and legal citation style vary considerably. For instance, legal citation gives only the author's last name, italicizes the article title, abbreviates journal titles, and puts the date near the end of the reference.

<182> Marjorie Jacobson, *Pregnancy and Employment: Three Approaches to Equal Opportunity*, 68 B.U.L. Rev. 1019 (1988) (LEXIS, Lawrev, Allrev).
- Refer to *A uniform system...* for periodical abbreviations.
- For a citation using APA style, see this reference and others in "Chapter Three: Full-Text Databases: Periodicals."

<183> Donald E. Lively & Stephen Plass, *Equal Protection: The Jurisprudence of Denial and Evasion*, 40 Am. U.L. Rev. 1307 (1991) (LEXIS, Lawrev, Allrev).
- An example with more than one author.

<184> Christopher D. Stone, *Beyond Rio: "Insuring" Against Global Warming*, 86 A.J.I.L. 445 (1992) (LEXIS, Lawrev, Allrev).

E. Rules, Regulations

1. Code of Federal Regulations

Basic Form

Name of Section, Title number C.F.R. Part number (date) (Give information sufficient for retrieval of item).

<185> Land and Water: Operation and Maintenance, 25 C.F.R. 171 (1992) (LEXIS, Codes, Cfr).
- For a citation using APA style, *see* entry 131.

2. Federal Register

Basic Form

Title or Name of the Section, volume Fed. Reg. page (date) (Give information sufficient for retrieval of item).

<186> Initial List of Categories of Sources under Section 112(c)(1) of the Clean Air Amendments of 1990, 57 Fed. Reg. 31576 (1992) (NEXIS, Exec, Fedreg).

  • For APA citation style, *see* entry 133.

F. U.S. Constitution

Basic Form

Constitution, article or amendment, section, paragraph, (date) (Give information sufficient for retrieval of item).

<187> U.S. Const. amend. 1, (1992) (FTP: oes.orst.edu Directory: bin/ compress File: us-const).

  • For a citation using APA style, *see* entry 149.

<188> U.S. Const. amend. 2, (1992) (LEXIS, Genfed, UScnst).

  • For citing the U.S. Constitution, source is not important as all sources will contain precisely the same part.
  • For a citation using APA style, *see* entry 150.

III. Numerical Databases

A. *Cite Part of a File*

Basic Form
Author. (date). Section. In *Title* [Type of medium]. Available: give information sufficient for retrieval of item from supplier.

<189> Income statement: quarterly report for 06/28/92. (1992, October 23). In *Starbucks Corp.* [Online]. Available: Dow-Jones News/ Retrieval Directory: DSCLO File: SBUX
   • If the database does not provide the date when the information was made available, give the date of the search in parentheses.

<190> Geographic segment data—1991. (1992, December 9). In *Nestle SA, Switzerland* [Online]. Available: NEXIS Library: COMPNY File: WLDSCP

<191> International Trade Administration. (1992, October 2). International securities transactions and offerings [Table 3]. In *U.S. industrial outlook, 1992* [Chapter 51, Security Firms], [CD-ROM]. Available: National Trade Data Bank—The Export Connection (R) Program: U.S. Industrial Outlook, 1992 Title: CHAP51 Securities Firms
   • If the source title does not indicate the contents clearly, give the program as a part of title.
   • When indicating availability, use the generic category names as they are used in the database. In this case, use "Program" and "Title" instead of "Directory" and "File."

<192> International Trade Administration. (1992, October 2). Key labor indicators. In *Foreign labor trends report: Hungary 1991–1992* [CD-ROM]. Available: National Trade Data Bank—The Export Connection (R) Program: Market Research Reports Title: Hungary—Foreign Labor Trends 1981–92—FLT9207

B. *Cite an Entire File in a Database*

Basic Form
Author. (date). *Title* (edition), [Type of medium]. Available: give information sufficient for retrieval of item from supplier.

<193> *Asian or Pacific Islander females* [CD-ROM]. (1990). Available: 1990 Census of Population and Housing Summary Tape File 3A Path: Vermont/Burlington, VT MSA/Race by sex by age File: Asian or Pacific Islander females

<194> Board of Governors of the Federal Reserve System. (1992, October 2). *Foreign spot exchange rate, Hong Kong* [Monthly Time Series, 1981–1991], [CD-ROM]. Available: National Trade Data Bank— The Export Connection (R) Program: Foreign Spot Exchange Rates Title: Foreign Spot Exchange Rates, Hong Kong
   • Here a government agency is the corporate author.
   • When indicating availability, use the generic category names as they are used in the database, in this example "Program" and "Title."

<195> Bureau of the Census. (1992. October 2). *Salmon, nesoi, fresh or chilled* [U.S. merchandise export trade, commodity by country], [CD-ROM]. Available: National Trade Data Bank—The Export Connection (R) Program: U.S. merchandise export trade, commodity by country Title: 0302120065—Salmon, nesoi, fresh or chilled

<196> *Japan, country profile* [Diskette]. (1992, October). Available: PC Globe Path: File/Output Country Data File: Japan

<197> *Nestle SA, Switzerland* (1992 report), [Online]. (1992, December 9). Available: NEXIS Library: COMPNY File: WLDSCP

<198> *[Nike] 1991 monthly summary* [Historical stock quotes], [Online]. (1992, November 5). Available: Dow Jones News/Retrieval Database: HQ File: nke 91 m
   • Word(s) supplied to make title more descriptive should be placed in brackets.

IV. Graphic Images: Charts, Maps, Photographs

Basic Form
Author (Function of the author). (date). *Title* [Type of medium]. Available:
   give information sufficient for location of item in source.

A. Charts

<199> *Electricity consumption* [Chart], [Diskette]. (1988). Available: PC
   Globe Path: Database/Comparison Charts File: Electricity Con-
   sumption
   • Since this entry does not have an author, the title is used as the
     first element of the entry.
   • The information in brackets describes the chart and enhances
     the information in the title.

<200> Gulf War vote, January 12, 1991 [Chart]. (1992). In *The almanac of
   American politics* [Online], p. 1477. Available: LEXIS Library:
   LEXREF File: AMPOL

B. Maps

<201> *Turkey: Elevations* [Map], [Diskette]. (1990, October). Available:
   PC Globe Path: Country/Elevations File: Turkey
   • Indicate the type of information in brackets following the title.
     In this case, the item is a map.

C. Photographs

<202> Bonnet, M. (Photographer). (1991). *Olympia, Bouleuterion: Section
   of entablature reconstructed at ground level on N side of S apsidal
   building* [Photograph], [Multimedia]. Available: Perseuse 1.0
   Path: Art and Archaeology/Architecture/Index by Site/
   Bouleuterion Card: Olympia, Bouleuterion
   • Give the function of the author or primary contributor(s) in pa-
     rentheses. In this example, the contributor is a photographer.
   • Indicate the type of information after the title.
   • Give the path taken to retrieve the information cited.

<203> Daniels, M. (Photographer). (1991). *Corinthian: Handle at right* [Photograph], [Multimedia]. Available: Perseuse 1.0 Path: Art and Archaeology/Pottery/Index by Collection/New Haven, Yale University Art Gallery Card: Yale 1988.80.37

V. Meeting Proceedings, Symposia

Basic Form
Author. (date, month day). Paper title. *Proceedings title* [Type of medium]. Available: give information sufficient for retrieval of article from supplier.

<204> Logan, H. (1992, September). Interactive art piece [Summary]. [Special issue devoted to fine art pieces and issues presented at SIGGRAPH '92]. *FINEART Forum* [Online], *6*(8). Available e-mail: fast@garnet.berkeley.edu
  • This is a citation to an electronic mail summary of proceedings that are published in an electronic journal.

<205> Perkins, S. C. (1992). *Indigenous peoples rights under international law* [Online]. Paper presented at the 1992 Annual Meeting of the American Association of Law Libraries. Available Telnet: liberty.uc.wlu.edu Select: to legal sources File: Perkins, Researching indigenous...
  • Capitalize the name of a symposium, which is a proper name.
  • Once a user gets to the Telnet site, an action is selected which results in the location of a file.

VI. Theses/Dissertations

A. Cite Part of a Work

Basic Form
Author. (date). Section. *Title of thesis/dissertation* (Master's thesis/Doctoral dissertation, University), [Type of medium]. Available: give information sufficient for retrieval of item from supplier.

<206> Strangelove, M. (1992). Josephus, Aliturus and Poppea Sabina. In *Patron-client dynamics in Flurius Josephus' VITA: A cross-*

> *disciplinary analysis* (Master's thesis, University of Ottawa), [On-
> line]. Available FTP: 137.122.6.16 Directory: pub/religion File:
> strangelove-thesis-part3.ps.Z
>   • Give the country name if the university is not identifiable.

B. Cite an Entire Work

Basic Form

Author. (date). *Title of Thesis/Dissertation* (Master's thesis/Doctoral dissertation, University), [Type of medium]. Available: give information
sufficient for retrieval of item from supplier.

<207> Strangelove, M. (1992). *Patron-client dynamics in Flarius Jose-
phus' VITA: A cross-disciplinary analysis* (Master's thesis, University of Ottawa, Canada), [Online]. Available FTP: 137.122.6.16
Directory: pub/religion File: Josephus.Zip
   • Give the country name if the university is not identifiable.

VII. Transcripts (Radio and Television) and Wire Service Reports

A. Radio and Television Transcripts

Basic Form

Author or reporter. (date). Title/Topic [Kind of transcript]. *Source* [Type of
medium]. Available: give information sufficient for retrieval of the item.

<208> King, L. (1992, December 10). [Television transcript of King's in-
terview with former President Jimmy Carter]. *CNN: Larry King
Live* [Online]. Available: NEXIS Library: NEXIS File: SCRIPT
   • This item has no title, so the descriptive information in brackets is used as the title.
   • Capitalize the names of radio or television shows, which are
   proper names.

<209> Koppel, T. (1992, October 21). Los Angeles revisited, Part one [Tel-
evision transcript]. *ABC News: Nightline* [Online]. Available:
NEXIS Library: NEXIS File: ABCNEW

<210> Neary, L. (1992, September 23). Children and the war with Iraq [Ra-
dio transcript]. *NPR: All Things Considered* [Online]. Available:
NEXIS Library: NEXIS File: NPR

<211> Simon, S. (1992, June 27). Mobutu retains complete control of Zaire [Radio transcript]. *NPR: Weekend Edition* [Online]. Available: NEXIS Library: NEXIS File: SCRIPT

B. Wire Service Reports

Basic Form
Author or byline. (date). Title. *Source* [Type of medium]. Available: give information sufficient for retrieval of the item.
  • The "source" is the name of the wire service.

<212> Pullella, P. (1992, December 25). Pope condemns "programmed" violence in Bosnia. *Reuters, Ltd.* [Online]. Available: NEXIS Library: NEXIS File: INTL

<213> Sophia Loren named "refugee ambassador" to Kenya and Somalia. (1992, October 30). *Agence France Presse* [Online]. Available: NEXIS Library: NEXIS File: WIRES

<214> U.S. aircraft start airlifting food to Somalia and Kenya. (1992, August 21). *Xinhua General Overseas News Service* [Online]. Available: NEXIS Library: NEXIS File: XINHUA

VIII. Entire Full-Text Databases

Basic Form
Database [Type of medium]. (Inclusive date). Place: Producer. Available: Distributor File:

<215> *Mental Measurement Yearbook* [Online]. (1972–). Lincoln, NE: Buros Institute of Mental Measurements. Available: BRS/After Dark File: Mental Measurements Yearbook (MMYD)

<216> *New York Times* [Online]. (1980, June–). N.Y.: New York Times Company. Available: LEXIS/NEXIS Library: NEXIS File: NYT

<217> *OAG—Official Airline Guides Electronic Edition Travel Service* [Online]. (Current). Oak Brook, IL: Official Airline Guide, Inc. Available: DIALOG File: OAG
  • This example shows the database is updated constantly and no date is given.

Chapter Five:
Bibliographic Databases

I. Cite an Abstract from a Database

A. Abstract of a Monograph or Individual Work

Basic Form
Author. (date). *Title* [Type of medium]. Abstract from: give information
sufficient for retrieval of abstract from database.

<218> *Burundi biological diversity and tropical forest assessment* [Dis-
kette]. (1989, January). Abstract from: The 1990 Directory of
Country Environmental Studies Program: Tropical Forest and Bio-
logical Diversity Assessments—USAID
  • If the author is not available, use the title as the first element
    of the entry.

<219> Lewis, R. C. (1980). *A discriminant analysis approach to group seg-
mentation of restaurant patronage based on advertising appeals*
[Abstract of doctoral dissertation, University of Chicago, 1980],
[Online]. Abstract from: DIALOG File: Dissertation Abstracts
Online (35) Item: 692187

<220> Rodriguez, A. M. (1991). *Multicultural education: Some considera-
tions for a university setting* [Online]. Abstract from: SilverPlat-
ter's ERIC Item: ED337094

B. Abstract of a Journal Article

Basic Form
Author. (year, month). Title [Type of medium]. *Journal, volume* (issue).
Abstract from: give information sufficient for retrieval of abstract from da-
tabase.

<221> Clinton, B. (1992, November). A technology policy for America:
Six broad initiatives [Online]. *EFFector Online, 3*(8). E-mail ab-

stract from: PACS-L@UHUPVM1 Subject: Current Cites 3, no. 11 (Part 11)

- Example of an abstract from a remote source (e-mail).

<222> Ohata, T., Honda, K., Hirata, S., Tamamura, K., Ishikawa, H., Miyahara, K., Mori, Y., & Kojima, C. (1986, September). AlGaAs/ GaAs distributed feedback laser diodes grown by MOCVD [Online]. *Journal of Crystal Growth*, 77(1–3). Abstract from: DIALOG File: INSPEC (12, 13) Item: 722477

- List all of the authors given.

C. Abstract of a Magazine Article

Basic Form
Author. (year, month day). Title [Type of medium]. *Magazine.* Abstract from: give information sufficient for retrieval of abstract from database.

<223> Cloud, D. S. (1992, September 26). Trade: Will NAFTA prove a policy prophecy? [Online]. *Congressional Quarterly Weekly Report.* Abstract from: Expanded Academic Index

<224> Green, P. S. (1989, October 23). Fashion colonialism: French export "Marie Claire" makes in-roads [CD-ROM]. *Advertising Age.* Abstract from: ABI/INFORM Item: 89–41770

D. Abstract of a Newspaper Article

Basic Form
Author or byline. (year, month day). Title [Type of medium]. *Newspaper.* Abstract from: give information sufficient for retrieval of abstract from database.

<225> Barmash, I. (1989, February 2). Talking deals: Dillard's desire for Vendex stake [Online]. *New York Times.* Abstract from: DIALOG File: Courier Plus (484) Item: 00002042

II. Cite Part of a Bibliographic Database

Basic Form
Part (Full name if given). (Inclusive dates). *Database* [Type of medium].
Place: Producer. Available: Distributor File:
- It is important to give producer and location of producer when citing all or part of a database.

<226> EN (Energy). (1986–1992). *Enviro/Energyline Abstracts Plus* [CD-ROM]. New York: R. R. Bowker (Producer). Available: R. R. Bowker File: EN

<227> ERIC CIJE (Current Index to Journals in Education). (1969–). *ERIC* [Online]. Washington, DC: Educational Resources Information Center (Producer). Available Telnet: uvm.carl.org Directory: ERIC File: ERIC CIJE

<228> ERIC RIE (Resources in Education). (1966–). *ERIC* [Online]. Washington, DC: Educational Resources Information Center (Producer). Available: DIALOG File: ERIC (1)

III. Cite an Entire Bibliographic Database

Basic Form
Database [Type of medium]. (Inclusive dates). Place: Producer. Available: Distributor File:

<229> *ABI/INFORM* [Online]. (1971–). Louisville: UMI/Data Courier (Producer). Available: DIALOG File: ABI/INFORM (15)
- Give the producer if different from the distributor.

<230> *AGRICOLA* [CD-ROM]. (1970–1978). Beltsville: National Agricultural Library (Producer). Available: SilverPlatter
- This database is comprised of only one file, so the "File" segment in the availability statement is not necessary.

<231> *ProQuest: ABI/INFORM On Disc* [CD-ROM]. (January, 1987–December 1989). Louisville: UMI (Producer).
- Cite only the producer if it is the direct supplier of the database.

Chapter Six:
Electronic Conferences (Interest Groups) or Bulletin Board Services (BBS)

I. Cite a Message

Basic Form
Author of message. (year, month day). Subject of message. *Electronic Conference or BBS* [Online]. Available e-mail: LISTSERV@e-mail address

<232> Hurst, J. A. (1992, September 10). International finance questions. *Business Libraries Discussion List* [Online]. Available e-mail: BUSLIB-L@IDBSU.BITNET
- Capitalize the names of discussion groups, and lists as they are proper names.

<233> SAUNDERG. (1992, September 21). Origin(s) of race. *General Anthropology Bulletin Board* [Online]. Available e-mail: ANTHRO-L@BVM.BITNET
- In many cases, the message is unsigned. In those instances, use the author's log-in name in uppercase letters.

II. Cite a Discussion or Conference: One Topic, Several Discussants

Basic Form
Author of message. (year, month day). Topic of discussion [Discussion]. *LISTSERV* [Online]. Available e-mail: LISTSERV@e-mail address

<234> Bell, S. (1992, September 16). Population projections [Discussion]. *Business Libraries Discussion List* [Online]. Available e-mail: BUSLIB-L@IDBSU.BITNET
- Include "[discussion]" to indicate that this message is from a discussion.

<235> CHRISTIN. (1992, September 22). HRAF/Librarian spouses [Discussion]. *General Anthropology Bulletin Board* [Online]. Available e-mail: ANTHRO-L@UBVM.BITNET
- If the author's name is not available, use the author's log-in name in uppercase letters.

<236> Silberger, K. (1992, September 15). Population projections [Discussion]. *Business Libraries Discussion List* [Online]. Available e-mail: BUSLIB-L@IDBSU.BITNET

III. Cite a Forwarded Message (BBS)

Basic Form
Person forwarding the message. (year, month day). Subject of message. Original sender of message, *Forwarded subject of message* [Online]. Available e-mail: LISTSERV@e-mail Address

<237> Crane, N. (1992, November 30). Malcolm X. Original sender M. Meeropol, *X* [Online]. Available e-mail: AFAM-L%MIZZOOT.BITNET
- Give the person who forwards the message as the author.

<238> Ross, L. (1992, September 16). New source guide. Original sender M. Strangelove (1992, September 14), *Electric mystic's guide draft 10* [Online]. Available e-mail: PACS-L@UHUPVM1.BITNET
- If the date of the original message is different from the forwarding date, give the date after the original sender's name.

IV. Cite an Entire Electronic Conference (Interest Group) or Bulletin Board Service (BBS)

Basic Form
LISTSERV [Type of medium]. Available e-mail: LISTSERV@e-mail address

<239> *Alcoholic & Drug Studies* [Online]. Available e-mail: ALCOHOL@LMUACAU.BITNET

<240> *Algeria News List* [Online]. Available e-mail: ALG-
NEWS@GWUVM.BITNET

<241> *Forum on Risks to the Public in Computers and Related Systems* [On-
line]. Available e-mail: risksrequest@csl.sri.com

V. Usenet Messages: Multiple Topics and Discussants

Basic Form
Author. (year, month day). *Subject* [Discussion], [Online]. Available e-
mail: USENET Newsgroup: name of the group

<242> Palo, G. (1993, January 7). *The Taj Mahal is a Hindu temple* [Dis-
cussion], [Online]. Available e-mail: USENET Newsgroup:
soc.history

<243> Reynolds, S. (1993, January 8). *Concerned about lone Canada
Goose* [Discussion], [Online]. Available e-mail: USENET Newsgroup: rec.birds

<244> Tranholm, S. (1993, January 8). *2001: A space odyssey* [Discus-
sion], [Online]. Available e-mail: USENET Newsgroup: alt.cult-
movies

Chapter Seven:
Electronic Mail (Personal)

I. Correspondence

Basic Form
Author. (year, month day). *Subject of the message* [e-mail to recipient's name], [Online]. Available e-mail: recipient's e-mail address

<245> Corliss, B. (1992, September 16). *News from Seattle* [e-mail to X. Li], [Online]. Available e-mail: XLI@UVMVM.UVM.EDU

II. Forwarded Mail with Embellishments

Basic Form
Forwarder. (year, month day). Subject of the forwarded message. *Subject of the original message* [forwarder's e-mail to recipient from originator, date], [Online]. available e-mail: recipient's e-mail address

<246> Archdeacon, D. (1992, October 30). Update on Latvia. *Life in the Baltics* [D. Archdeacon's forwarded e-mail to N. Crane from M. Saule, October 27, 1992], [Online]. Available e-mail: NCRANE@uvmvm.uvm.edu

<247> Emerson, T. (1992, August 24). *Second version of queues at information desks* [T. Emerson's forwarded e-mail to R. Leer from T. Bolling, August 11, 1992], [Online]. Available e-mail: rleer@yorkvm1
  • This forwarded message came without a forwarder's added "subject of message" so the subject of the original message is cited directly after the date.

Chapter Eight:
Computer Programs

Basic Form

Author. (date). *Name of program* (version), [Computer program]. Available: give information sufficient for retrieval of the program.

<248> Holmes, R. D. & Kidd, K. K. (no date). *POPGEN: Population genetics simulation package* (DOS version 2.0), [Computer program]. Available Distributor: R. D. Holmes, New Haven, CT (Department of Human Genetics, Yale University, 333 Cedar St., Zip: 06510).
   • For items of limited circulation, include the address of the distributor in parentheses.

<249> *MacConcord I (KJV)* (Apple MacIntosh version 1.2), [Computer program]. (no date). Available Distributor: Medina Software, Longwood, FL Order no.: 48842–500

<250> Wu, A. H. & Jenkins, B. (1990, May 1). *Diagnostic ordering in clinical medicine* (DOS version 1.0), [Computer program]. Available Distributor: Health Sciences Consortium, Chapel Hill, NC (Address: 201 Silver Cedar Court, Zip: 27514).

Chapter Nine:
Reference Citations in Text

The system of documentation recommended by the APA is called the author-date system. References in the text direct readers to the source of a quotation or work under discussion in the alphabetic reference list at the end of an article, chapter, or book. This appendix gives some of the more common examples of "in-text citation."

I. A Work by a Single Author

Lewis Carroll's *Alice's adventures...* (1991) is available at an FTP site...

Classic works, such as *Alice's adventures in wonderland* (Carroll, 1991), are now available...

II. A Work by Two or More Authors

Girotti, Tweed, and Houser (1990) found real-time VAr control...

In subsequent references, the above may be cited as follows: Girotti et al. (1990) have continued earlier work...

If the work being cited has six or more authors, cite only the first author followed by "et al." For example, a work by Kutner, Li, Mardeusz, Philbin, Reit, Day, Barickman, Ross, Robertson, and Crane published in 1992 would be cited as (Kutner et al., 1992).

III. A Work by a Corporate Author

Generally the names of corporate authors are spelled out in full in the text reference:

The National Aids Information Clearinghouse guidelines (1988) give explicit...

For corporate authors with lengthy names, subsequent references may be abbreviated:

(NAIC, 1988)

IV. Works When No Author is Given

When an item in the reference list has no author, cite the first three or four words of the title of the work:

Researchers report in "Exercise helps clear fat," (1990) that heart patients...

The new edition of *Birth defects encyclopedia online* (1992)...

V. References to a Specific Part of a Source

Heshusius, in his response to Dixon and Carnine, says "... " (1992, p. 472).

The first entry in *Birth defects encyclopedia online*, sets the pattern for subsequent entries... (1992, p. 1).

References

Gibaldi, J. (1988). *The MLA handbook for writers of research papers* (3rd ed.). New York: Modern Language Association of America.

Labaton, S. (1993, January 8). Preserving history, and trivia, in computer files. *New York Times*, Late Edition, Law Page, Sec. B, p. 14. Available: NEXIS Library: NEXIS File: NYT

Marcaccio, K. Y. (Ed.). (1992). *Computer readable databases*. Detroit: Gale.

Publication manual of the American Psychological Association (3rd ed). (1983). Washington, DC: American Psychological Association.

Strangelove, M. & Kovacs, D. (1992). *Directory of electronic journals, newsletters and academic discussion lists* (2nd. ed.). Washington, D. C.: Association of Research Libraries.

A uniform system of citation (15th ed.). (1991). Cambridge, MA: Harvard Law Review Association.

Basic Availability Statements for Commonly Used Electronic Information Sources

The following electronic information suppliers/sources are ones that are in fairly wide use. This appendix gives the standard form of the available statement for each supplier, and where possible, gives examples for citing a *whole* work or database, and for citing *part* of a work (i.e., a chapter, journal article).

Commercial Sources

BRS
(whole): Available: BRS File: National College Databank (PETE)
(part): Available: BRS File: ABI Inform Item: 00591201

BRS/After Dark
(whole): Available: BRS/After Dark File: Birth Defects Encyclopedia Online (BDEO)
(part): Available: Mental Measurements Yearbook (MMYD) Item: 1012–327

DIALOG
(whole): Available: DIALOG File: Social Scisearch (7)
(part): Available: DIALOG File: Health Periodicals Database (149) Item: 915010

Dow Jones News Retrieval Service
(part): Available: Dow Jones News Retrieval Service Directory: DSCLO File: SBUX

Information Access Company (CD-ROM)
(whole): Available: Information Access Company (INFOTRAC) File: Health Information Center

Knowledge Index
(whole): Available: Knowledge Index File: Agrochemicals Handbook (CHEM3)
(part): Available: Knowledge Index File: Kirk-Othmer Online (CHEM5) Item: 323270000

LEXIS/NEXIS
(whole): Available: NEXIS Library: OMNI
(part): Available: LEXIS Library: LEXREF File: AMPOL

University Microfilms (UMI)
(part): Available: UMI File: Business Periodicals Ondisc Item: 92–13721

University Publications of America
(part): Available: University Publications of America File: Scholarly Book Reviews on CD-ROM

WESTLAW
(part): Available: WESTLAW File: US-PL

Ziff Communications Co. (CD-ROM)
(part): Available: Ziff Communications Co. File: Computer Select Item: 12 235 992

Non-commercial Sources

Electronic Mail (e-mail)
(part): Available e-mail: NISINFO@NIS.NSF.NET Message: Get RFC1175.TXT-1

FTP
(part): Available FTP: quake.think.com Directory: pub/etext/1991 File: alice-in-wonderland.txt

Telnet
(part): Available Telnet: Library. Dartmouth.edu Directory: Shakespeare Plays File: Hamlet

Glossary

This glossary defines terms which might be unfamiliar to new users of electronic information, or which might have taken on new shades of meaning for the purposes of this guide. Words given in boldface type in the definitions are also defined in this glossary.

Author. A person or corporate body responsible for the contents of a work.

Available. In the context of this guide, available is used to inform the reader where to locate and how to retrieve electronic information from a supplier. See Appendix I for examples of availability statements used in this guide.

CD-ROM (Compact Disc Read-Only Memory). A compact disc that stores text, data, graphics and sound. A single CD-ROM disc can hold up to 250,000 pages of text. It is widely used as an alternative to **online** sources for the dissemination of information.

Corporate Author. An organization having responsibility for the content of a publication, for example a government body, a business entity, or an association.

Directory. In the context of this guide, a **directory** serves as a contents listing of a collection of **files.**

Discussion Group. A group of people, often with a common interest, registered with a central computer for the purpose of conversing about that interest. Their conversations are stored and made available to all of the registrants via **e-mail.**

Diskette. A removable, magnetic disk that stores varying amounts of information depending on the storage parameters of the diskette. (Also called a floppy disk.)

E-mail. This is a commonly used abbreviation for **electronic mail.**

Electronic Mail. A computerized mail system that allows an individual to send messages to another individual or a group.

File. A definable collection of data held on an electronic or magnetic storage device.

FTP. (File Transfer Protocol). FTP allows for the transfer of **files** from one computer to another via a network.

Full-Length Work. A complete and independent work that is retrievable as a unit.

Full-text. The text of a complete document stored so that it can be retrieved electronically.

Internet. Linking, high-speed networks (campus, state, regional, national, and international) sharing standardized communications protocols (TCP/IP) and common address parameters.

LISTSERV. See **Discussion Group.**

Message. In the context of this guide, it is a request sent to a **discussion group** or **LISTSERV** to get a **file.**

Multimedia. An electronic source that incorporates text, graphics, moving images, and sound.

Online. In the context of this guide, an online format implies that stored information is retrievable in a real-time, interactive manner.

Path. Route taken to locate and retrieve a **file.**

Telnet. An **Internet** protocol allowing remote terminals to connect and interact with a time-sharing system.

Index

References are made to entry numbers unless otherwise noted.

Creo que casi todo el mundo conoce estos mecanismos. Veamos el siguiente ejemplo: nos proponemos alimentarnos de un modo más consciente y perder peso. Por eso hemos llenado la despensa y la nevera de alimentos sanos y nutritivos. Comenzamos el día haciendo ejercicio y disfrutamos con la magnífica sensación que esto produce en nuestro organismo.

Al cabo de muy poco tiempo ocurre entonces lo siguiente: nos resfriamos o sufrimos una herida, lo que nos impide seguir debidamente con el programa de ejercicios. O nos invitan a una fiesta y no sabemos decir que no cuando nos ofrecen una bebida alcohólica o un postre de chuparse los dedos. Tal vez la cosa no se limite entonces a una cerveza y una mousse de chocolate, por no hablar de otros platos que podríamos aplicarnos directamente a las caderas, por mucho que en casa nos hubiéramos propuesto permanecer firmes por esta vez.

El motivo de esta «recaída» se halla en las sinapsis (uniones entre neuronas) de nuestro cerebro, que a lo largo de la vida se han activado tantas veces que en determinadas situaciones reaccionamos siempre de la misma manera. Para cambiar estos automatismos y crear nuevas sinapsis que nos ayuden a alcanzar nuestros objetivos, es preciso que durante 28 días operemos continuamente con una «nueva» programación. La investigación ha demostrado que para romper con una pauta antigua y programar otra más positiva se necesitan de 21 a 28 días. Entonces se forman nuevas vías neuronales en el cerebro y con ellas otras creencias favorables a la vida.

Mientras estaba yo meditando con los ángeles en Maui (Hawái), ellos me aconsejaron que elaboráramos juntos un programa de 28 días para ayudar a las personas a alcanzar sus metas. La idea me entusiasmó desde el primer momento, pues no en vano yo misma había obtenido ya efectos maravillosos y trasformaciones fantásticas con programas de este tipo.

Por ejemplo, hace diez años estuve trabajando con el libro *El camino del artista*, de Julia Cameron, que propone un programa de tres meses (!) con tareas diarias. Entonces todavía estaba yo muy